being poor

by Janet Rosenberg
illustrations by Nancy Inderieden

CAROLRHODA BOOKS
MINNEAPOLIS, MINNESOTA U.S.A.

To Miriam and Ruth

All rights reserved. International copyright secured.
Manufactured in the United States of America. Published
simultaneously in Canada by J. M. Dent & Sons Ltd.,
Don Mills, Ontario.

International Standard Book Number 0-87614-036-3
Library of Congress Catalog Card Number 72-7658

Second Printing 1975

being poor

being poor is...

wearing a spring coat in winter.

being poor is...

taking turns going to school because you have to share your sister's boots.

being poor is...

   having your heat shut off in freezing weather because your mother can't pay the bill.

being poor is...

       having two blankets for seven people in the family.

being poor is...

wanting to feel proud of your father because he has a job—but he can't find work.

being poor is...

wishing you could eat in a restaurant.

being poor is...

wishing you could have meat whenever you want it.

being poor is...

       wearing shoes that someone else threw out.

being poor is...

the sad look on your mother's face when you need school clothes.

being poor is...

buying an old coat at a second-hand store and feeling lucky.

INSTITUTE FOR JUSTICE AND PEACE
WALSH COLLEGE CANTON, OH 44720

being poor is...

  having to do your homework by
a 40-watt light bulb.

being poor is...

riding three buses to a clinic
when you're feeling sick.

being poor is...

waiting all day in a clinic to see
a doctor you don't know.

being poor is...

a welfare worker asking your mother too many questions and making her cry.

being poor is...

a scout troop dropping a Christmas basket at your door.

being poor is...

pretending you don't care when you don't get any Christmas presents.

being poor is...

      not being afraid of a dentist because you've never seen one.

being poor is...

      not being able to buy toothpaste.

being poor is...

borrowing paper in school and promising to pay it back but knowing you'll never be able to.

being poor is...

feeling ashamed because you can't afford the school movie.

being poor is...

always feeling a little mad
because you never have what you need.

About the Author

Janet Rosenberg received her Master's Degree in social work at Smith College. Since then she has had many years of experience in giving direct service to the poor. Mrs. Rosenberg's work has taken her into poverty areas as a street worker, and into the classroom to teach social workers how to understand and help the poor. In 1969, her book, BREAKFAST: TWO JARS OF PASTE, received national attention as a text for workers in the human service field. At the present time, Mrs. Rosenberg is completing work toward a Ph.D. at Case Western Reserve University in Cleveland, Ohio, where she also conducts research at the Cleveland Veteran's Hospital and serves as a parent counselor at an experimental Drop-In Center at the Cleveland Jewish Family Service.

BEING POOR expresses the author's commitment to the idea that if children know about the adverse conditions of poverty, they will develop a desire to change these conditions.

About the Artist

Nancy Inderieden's amusing and fanciful illustrations have appeared in many books for children, including THE DIRTY BOY, ROBBIE'S FRIEND GEORGE, THE BRIDGE TO BLUE HILL, and ALL ALONG THE WAY. In BEING POOR, Nancy shows her versatile talent by capturing the book's serious mood with her stark yet sensitive black-and-white drawings.

Nancy Inderieden received her training at the Minneapolis College of Art and Design. Today, she combines a career of graphic design and illustration with photography and portrait work. Nancy, her husband, and four children live in a rural community near Stillwater, Minnesota.

CAROLRHODA BOOKS
241 FIRST AVENUE NORTH — MINNEAPOLIS, MINNESOTA 55401

Published in memory of Carolrhoda Locketz Rozell,
Who loved to bring children and books together

Please write for a complete catalogue